# Companion notebook

## cycle two
-fifth edition compatible-

### weeks 13-24

copyright 2019 by Amy Atkins

No part of this book may be reproduced in an form for by any electronic
or mechanical means without prior written permission from the publisher
except that one family may make individual copies for personal home
educational use.

Printed in the United States.

The Foundations Guide and all memory work is copyrighted by Classical Conversations, Inc.
Their textbook materials are required for the completion of these worksheets.
This notebook is all fill-in-the-blank and cannot replace their material.

All rights reserved.

Design & Content: Amy Atkins

Editing: Sunshine & Oranges Editing Team

Sunshine & Oranges
www.sunshineandorages.com

# *acknowledgements*

To our Lord and Creator who created us in His image
so therefore we find the need to create.
To our children, the reason for these notebooks, each also
made in His image.
To our husbands, for their love and support.
To our friends, who test our pages and listen to our crazy ideas.
To you, for buying this journal and enjoying it.

## DOWNLOADS SUBSCRIPTION

Join our download membership to download any of these pages, and more, on demand at any time.
sunshineandoranges.com/downloads

## BLOG

Devotionals, encouragement, and ideas all in one place...
our blog!
sunshineandoranges.com/blog

## SHOP

Get some science cards, bible study cards, and more!
sunshineandoranges.com/shop

Questions or Suggestions:
Amy Atkins
amy@sunshineandoranges.com


Don't forget to sign up for our newsletter for news
and new products to help your homeschooling journey.

# Week 13

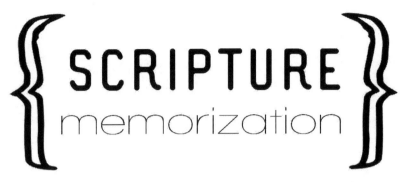

Find a verse in the Bible in your translation of choice.
Write it, say it, pray it, and memorize it.

**WRITE IT:** _____

_____

_____

_____

**SAY IT.**

**PRAY IT.**

**WRITE IT AGAIN (FROM MEMORY)** _____

_____

_____

_____

_____

# ENGLISH week 13

## More Indefinite Pronouns

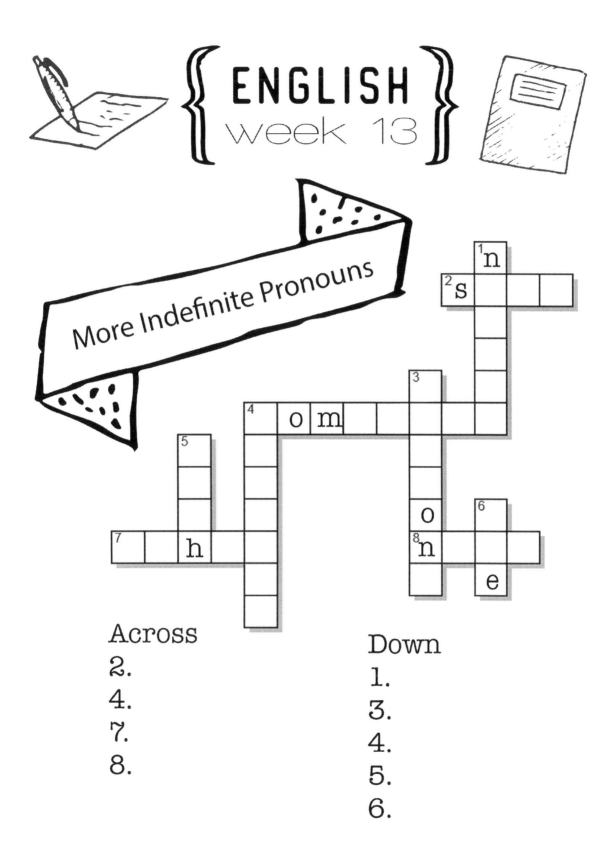

Across
2.
4.
7.
8.

Down
1.
3.
4.
5.
6.

Fill in the blanks for the history sentence this week and copy it below.

Tell me about the _____ _____.

_____ steam _____, _____ power _____, and _____ _____ gin _____ the _____ _____ that began in the _____.

_____
_____
_____
_____
_____
_____
_____

Research the history topic from this week. Write some notes below or draw a picture.

Write the geography locations of the week below.
Color the map to mark each location.

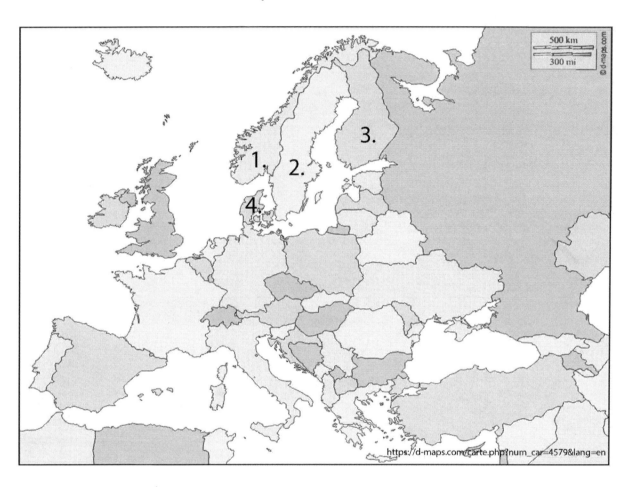

1.

2.

3.

4.

# 1st Conjugation Endings
# Present Tense

Sing the Latin Song for the week as you fill in the blanks

| singular | ___ ___ ___ | I<br>you<br>he, she, it |
|---|---|---|
| plural | ___ ___ ___ | we<br>you<br>they |

# Math
## week 13

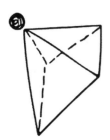 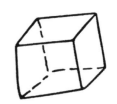

Write in the liquid equivalents.

___ fl. oz. = ___ c.

___ c. c. = ___ pt.

___ pt. pt. = ___ qt.

___ qt. qt. qt. qt. = ___ gal.

Solve the problems below.

2 gallons equals how many pints? _____
6 cups equals how many pints? _____
2 quarts equals how many cups? _____
2 pints equals how many fluid ounces? _____

Match the timeline events for the week with the correct year.

- c. 1400 to c. 1600
- c. 1419
- c. 1440
- c. 1455
- 1460
- 1462
- 1478

# SCIENCE
## U.S. space missions

Research and label the correct U.S. space mission on the timeline provided below.

1959-1963

6 Launched Crewed Missions
First U.S. Crewed Program

M_____

1963-1966

10 Launched Crewed Missions
Practiced space walks, docking, and more

G_____

1961-1972

6 Launched Crewed Missions
First Man on the Moon

A_____

1981-2011

135 Launched Crewed Missions

S_____

# Science research

Research the science topic from this week. Write some notes below or draw a picture.
_____

# REVIEW at a glance
## WEEK 13

## HISTORY
### TELL ME ABOUT...

## TIMELINE
1.
2.
3.
4.
5.
6.
7.

## GEOGRAPHY
1.
2.
3.
4.

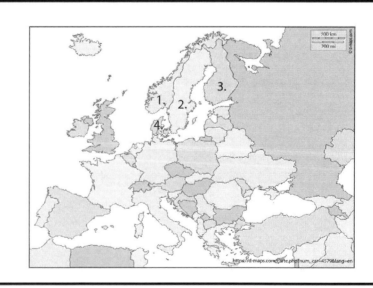

# REVIEW at a glance
## WEEK 13

**SCIENCE**

What are some names of U.S. space missions?

**MATH**

____ fluid ounces = 1 cup

____ cups = 1 pint

____ pints = 1 quart

____ quarts = 1 gallon

**ENGLISH**

What are some indefinite pronouns?

**LATIN**

1st Conjugation Endings

_____ Tense

| | singular | | |
|---|---|---|---|
| | -ō | I | |
| | -____ | you | |
| | -t | he, ____, it | |

| | plural | | |
|---|---|---|---|
| | -____ | we | |
| | -tis | you | |
| | -nt | ____ | |

# Week 14

# Journaling
date:

Find a verse in the Bible in your translation of choice.
Write it, say it, pray it, and memorize it.

**WRITE IT:** _____

_____

_____

_____

**SAY IT.**

**PRAY IT.**

**WRITE IT AGAIN (FROM MEMORY)** _____

_____

_____

_____

_____

## Adverbs

Fill in the blanks to make the definition of an adverb.

An _____ _____ a _____, _____, or another _____ - and answers the _____:

1.
2.
3.
4.

.................................................................

Dress up some verbs:

1. _____ ran

2. _____ walked

3. _____ talked

4. shouted _____

Fill in the blanks for the history sentence this week and copy it below.

Tell me about _____ _____ __ _____.
_____ of _____, _____ _____ of _____, _____ II of _____, _____ II of _____, and _____ of the _____ States were leaders during _____ ____ __, which started in _____ and _____ in _____.

_____
_____
_____
_____
_____
_____

Research the history topic from this week. Write some notes below or draw a picture.

Write the geography locations of the week below.
Color the map to mark each location.

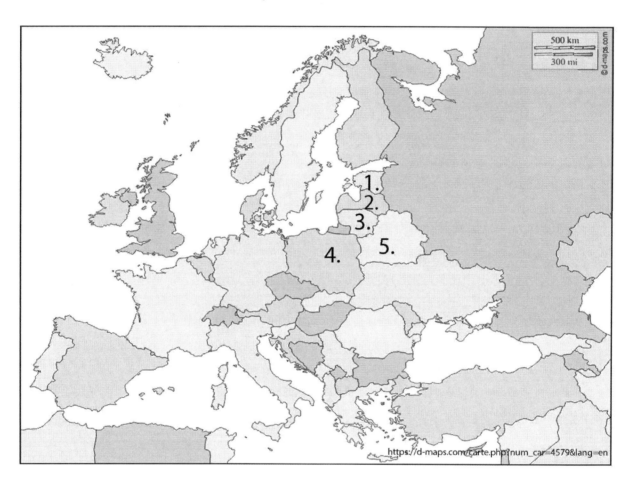

1.

2.

3.

4.

5.

## 1st Conjugation Endings
## Present Tense

Sing the Latin Song for the week as you fill in the blanks

| singular | ___ ___ ___ | I<br>you<br>he, she, it |
|---|---|---|
| plural | ___ ___ ___ | we<br>you<br>they |

# Math
## week 14

Write in the linear equivalents.

\_\_\_\_\_ = \_\_\_\_\_
centimeters     inch

\_\_\_\_\_ = \_\_\_\_\_
inches     foot

\_\_\_\_\_ = \_\_\_\_\_
feet     mile

\_\_\_\_\_ = \_\_\_\_\_
kilometer     mile

**Answer the questions below:**

How many inches is the length of the nearest table? _____

How many miles is it from your house to your favorite place to eat? _____

How many feet tall is the largest mountain in Alaska? _____

...and how many kilometers? _____

Match the timeline events for the week with the correct year.

1492

c. 1500 to c. 1800

1517

1519

1536

1545

c. 1600

Identify the states of matter using the diagram below and write them on the lines below the images.

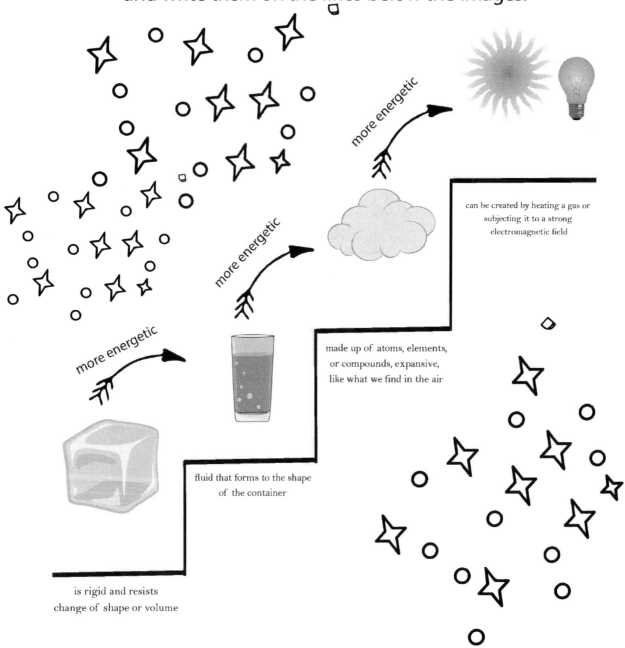

can be created by heating a gas or subjecting it to a strong electromagnetic field

made up of atoms, elements, or compounds, expansive, like what we find in the air

fluid that forms to the shape of the container

is rigid and resists change of shape or volume

Research the science topic from this week. Write some notes below or draw a picture.

# REVIEW at a glance
## WEEK 14

## HISTORY
TELL ME ABOUT...

## TIMELINE
1.
2.
3.
4.
5.
6.
7.

## GEOGRAPHY
1.
2.
3.
4.
5.

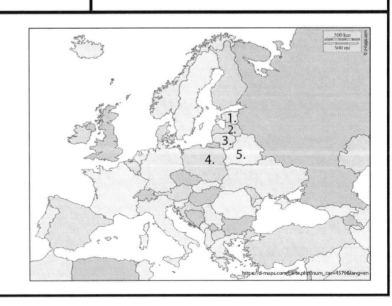

# REVIEW at a glance
## WEK 14

**SCIENCE** — What are the states of matter?

**MATH**

____ centimeters = 1 inch

____ inches = 1 foot

____ feet = 1 mile

1 kilometer =

**ENGLISH** — What is an adverb?

**LATIN**

1st Conjugation Endings
_____ Tense

|  | | |
|---|---|---|
| singular | -ō | I |
|  | -____ | you |
|  | -t | he, ____, it |
| plural | -____ | we |
|  | -tis | you |
|  | -nt | ____ |

# Week
## 15

Find a verse in the Bible in your translation of choice.
Write it, say it, pray it, and memorize it.

**WRITE IT:** _____

_____

_____

_____

**SAY IT.**

**PRAY IT.**

**WRITE IT AGAIN (FROM MEMORY)** _____

_____

_____

_____

_____

## FOUR PURPOSES OF SENTENCES

Fill in the blanks and match the sentences to the correct purpose.

D_____         Where is my chore list for today?

                           Take the first door on the right.

E_____         How I wish I were tall!

                           I am going to climb that fence.

I_____         Can you show me how?

                           Use this key to get in.

I_____         What a great writer you are!

                           I am going to make a pie you will love.

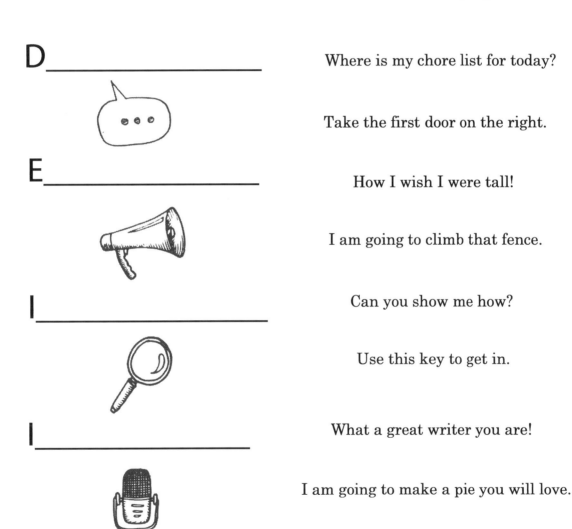

Fill in the blanks for the history sentence this week and copy it below.

Tell me about _____ \_\_\_\_ I _____.

During _____ \_\_\_\_\_ \_\_, Great _____, _____, and _____ were _____ and fought _____ _____-_____ and _____, which were called the _____ _____. In _____, the _____ _____ entered the war, _____ the _____.

_____

_____

_____

_____

Research the history topic from this week. Write some notes below or draw a picture.

Write the geography locations of the week below.
Color the map to mark each location.

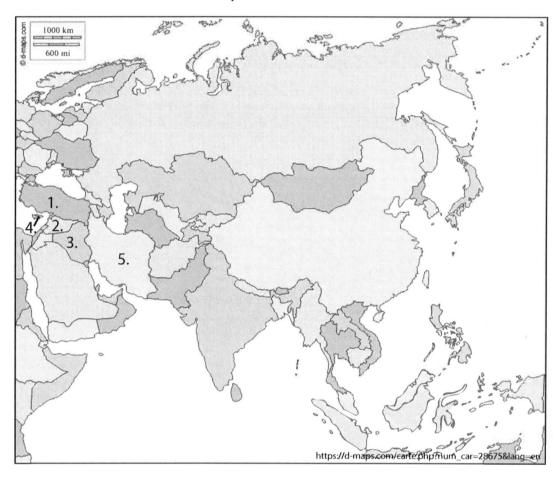

1.

2.

3.

4.

5.

# 1st Conjugation Endings
# Imperfect Tense

Sing the Latin Song for the week as you fill in the blanks

| singular | _____ _____ _____ | I was _ing<br><br>you were _ing<br><br>he, she, it was _ing |
|---|---|---|
| plural | _____ _____ _____ | we were _ing<br><br>you were _ing<br><br>they were _ing |

# Math
## week 15

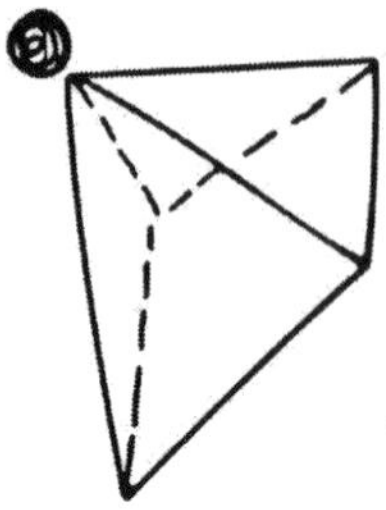

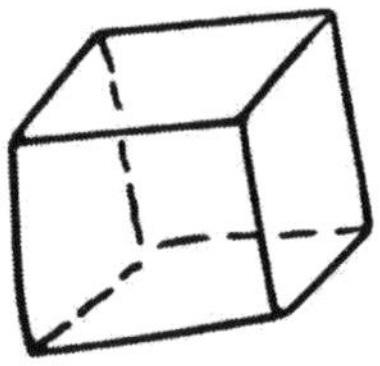

Write in the metric measurements.

____ millimeters = ____ centimeter

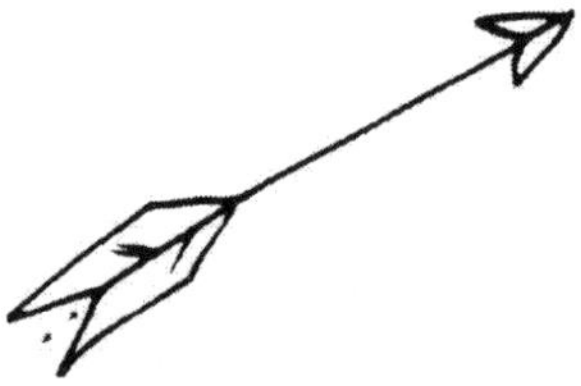

____ centimeters = ____ meter

____ meters = ____ kilometer

answer the questions below:

What is the abbreviation for centimeter? _____
What is the abbreviation for millimeter? _____
What is the abbreviation for meter? _____
What is the abbreviation for kilometer? _____
What is the abbreviation for mile? _____
What is the abbreviation for inch? _____

Match the timeline events for the week with the correct year.

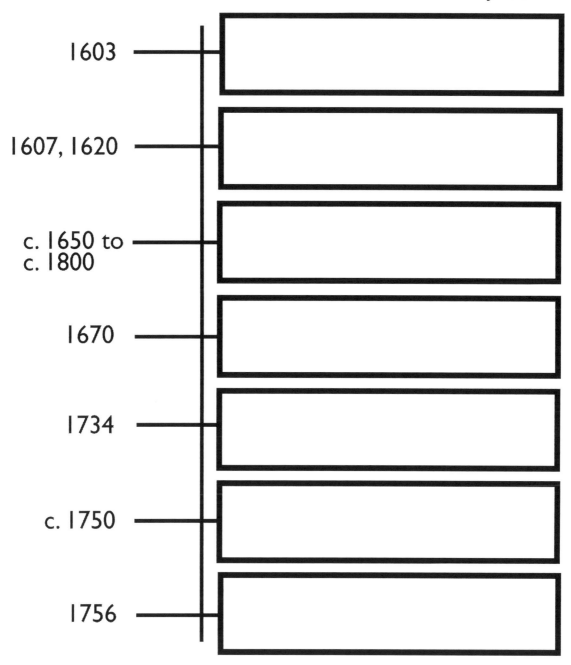

1603

1607, 1620

c. 1650 to c. 1800

1670

1734

c. 1750

1756

# SCIENCE
## Forms of energy

What are two forms of energy? Write them and draw examples of each.

---

energy which a body possesses by virtue of being in motion

---

the energy possessed by a body by virtue of its position relative to others, stresses within itself, electric charge, and other factors

Research the science topic from this week. Write some notes below or draw a picture.

# REVIEW at a glance
## WEEK 15

**HISTORY**
TELL ME ABOUT...

**TIMELINE**
1.
2.
3.
4.
5.
6.
7.

**GEOGRAPHY**
1.
2.
3.
4.
5.

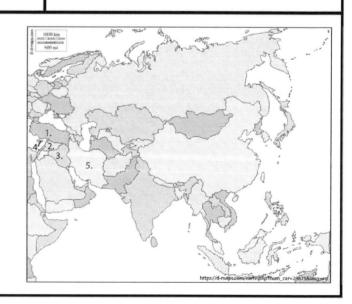

# REVIEW at a glance
## WEEK 15

**SCIENCE**
What are two forms of energy?

**MATH**
____ millimeters = 1 centimeter

____ centimeters = 1 meter

_____ meters = 1 kilometer

**ENGLISH**
Four purposes of sentences:

**LATIN**

1st Conjugation Endings
Imperfect Tense

| | | |
|---|---|---|
| singular | -  _ _ _ _ | I was _ing |
| | -  _ _ _ _ | you were _ing |
| | -  _ _ _ _ | he, she it was _ing |
| plural | -  _ _ _ _ _ _ | we were _ing |
| | -b_ _ _ _ _ | you were _ing |
| | -  _ _ _ _ | they were _ing |

# Week
## 16

Journaling

date:

Find a verse in the Bible in your translation of choice.
Write it, say it, pray it, and memorize it.

**WRITE IT:** _____

_____

_____

_____

**SAY IT.**

**PRAY IT.**

**WRITE IT AGAIN (FROM MEMORY)** _____

_____

_____

_____

# VERBS

Color the banners that match what a verb DOES. "X" the other boxes.

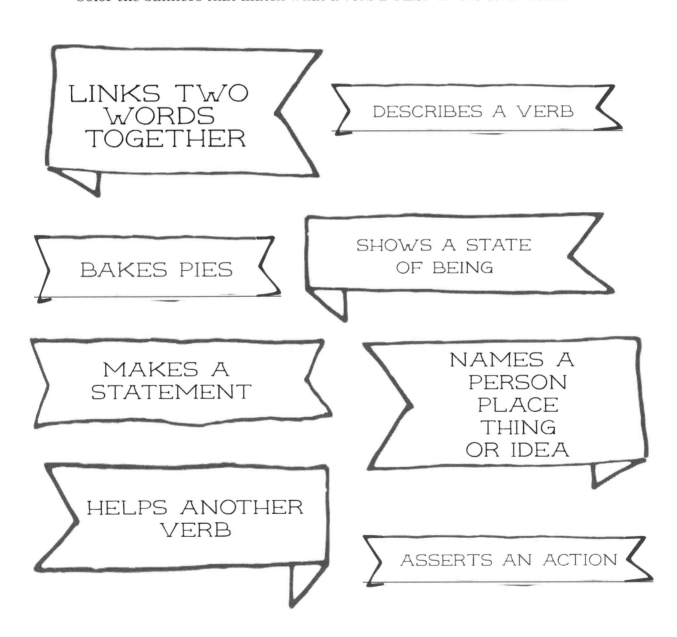

Fill in the blanks for the history sentence this week and copy it below.

Tell me about how _____ \_\_\_\_ \_\_ _____.

_____ War II began in _____ when _____ _____ _____. Two _____ that _____ the United _____ win the _____ front were _____ _____ at the _____ of _____ and _____ _____ _____ on _____ and _____ in _____.

_____

_____

_____

_____

_____

Research the history topic from this week. Write some notes below or draw a picture.

Write the geography locations of the week below.
Color the map to mark each location.

1.

2.

3.

4.

5.

  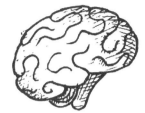

## 1st Conjugation Endings
## Imperfect Tense

Sing the Latin Song for the week as you fill in the blanks

| singular | ____ | I was _ing |
| | ____ | you were _ing |
| | ____ | he, she, it was _ing |
| plural | ____ | we were _ing |
| | ____ | you were _ing |
| | ____ | they were _ing |

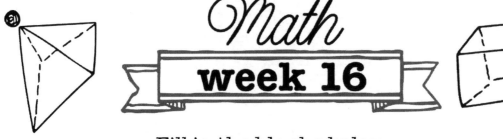

# Math
## week 16

Fill in the blanks below.

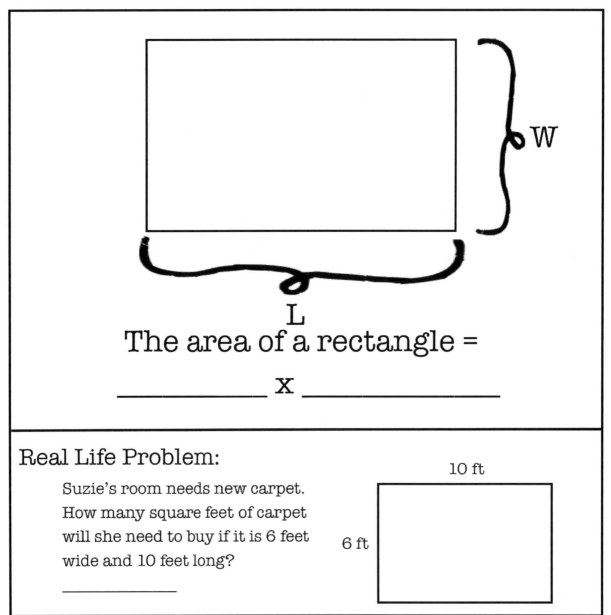

The area of a rectangle =

_____ x _____

### Real Life Problem:

Suzie's room needs new carpet. How many square feet of carpet will she need to buy if it is 6 feet wide and 10 feet long?

_____

10 ft

6 ft

Match the timeline events for the week with the correct year.

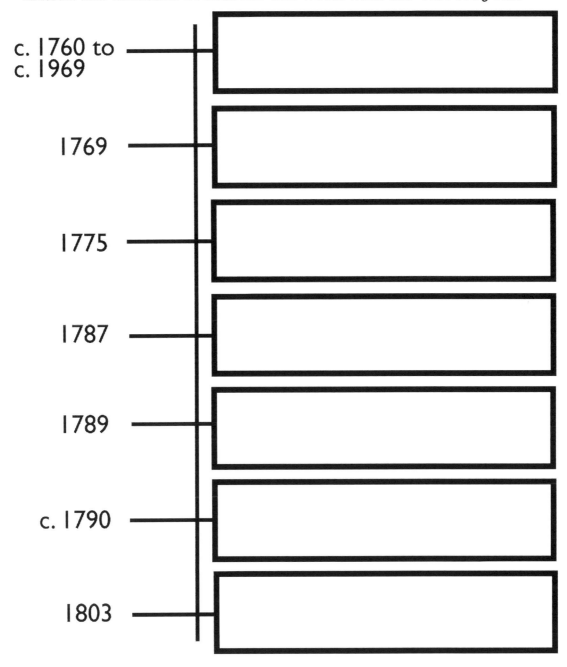

c. 1760 to c. 1969

1769

1775

1787

1789

c. 1790

1803

Recite and memorize Newton's First Law of Motion.
Make a comic strip below explaining it.

Research the science topic from this week. Write some notes below or draw a picture.

# REVIEW at a glance
## WEEK 16

**HISTORY**
TELL ME ABOUT...

**TIMELINE**
1.
2.
3.
4.
5.
6.
7.

**GEOGRAPHY**
1.
2.
3.
4.
5.

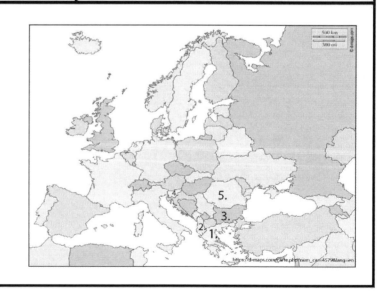

# REVIEW at a glance
## WEEK 16

**SCIENCE**: What is Newton's First Law of Motion?

**MATH**: What is the area of a rectangle?

**ENGLISH**: What is a verb?

**LATIN**:

1st Conjugation Endings
Imperfect Tense

| | singular | |
|---|---|---|
| | -_ _ _ _ | I was _ing |
| | -_ _ _ _ | you were _ing |
| | -_ _ _ _ | he, she it was _ing |

| | plural | |
|---|---|---|
| | -_ _ _ _ _ _ | we were _ing |
| | -b_ _ _ _ _ | you were _ing |
| | -_ _ _ _ _ | they were _ing |

# Week 17

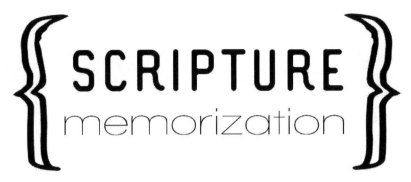

Find a verse in the Bible in your translation of choice.
Write it, say it, pray it, and memorize it.

**WRITE IT:** _____

_____

_____

_____

**SAY IT.**

**PRAY IT.**

**WRITE IT AGAIN (FROM MEMORY)** _____

_____

_____

_____

## NOUNS

Write 5 things a noun can name then write/draw an example noun in the banner.

1.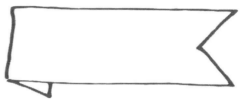

2.

3.

4.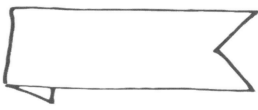

5.

Fill in the blanks for the history sentence this week and copy it below.

Tell me about _____ ____ II _____.

_____ ____ II _____ _____ were: _____ of _____, ____ of _____, and _____ of _____. _____ ____ II _____ _____ were: _____ of _____, _____, _____, and _____ of the _____ _____, and _____ of the _____.

_____

_____

_____

_____

_____

Research the history topic from this week. Write some notes below or draw a picture.

Write the geography locations of the week below.
Color the map to mark each location.

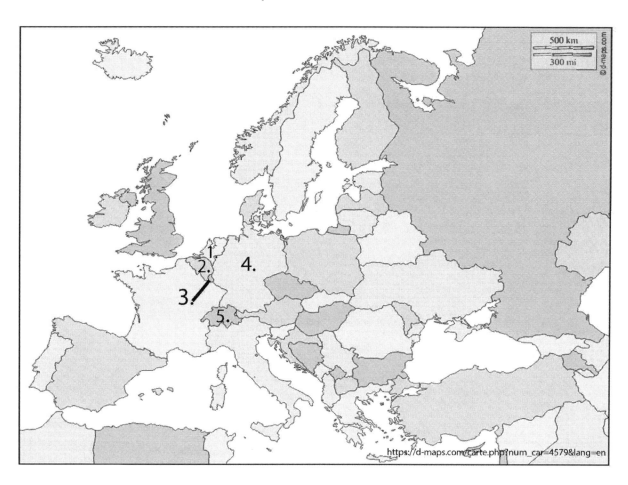

1.

2.

3.

4.

5.

  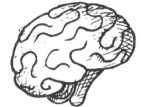

# 1st Conjugation Endings
# Future Tense

Sing the Latin Song for the week as you fill in the blanks

|  | |
|---|---|
| singular <br> _____ <br> _____ <br> _____ | I shall _ <br> you will _ <br> he, she, it will _ |
| plural <br> _____ <br> _____ <br> _____ | we shall _ <br> you will _ <br> they will _ |

# Math
## week 17

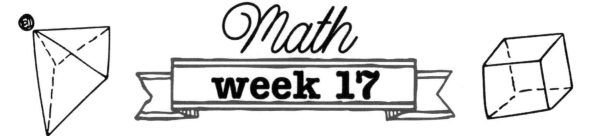

Fill in the blanks below.

}L

(remember: all sides of a square are equal)

The area of a square = the _____ of its _____ _____.

### Real Life Problem:

In Tyler's square box, he wants to cover the bottom with aluminum foil for a science experiement. He measured one side. It was 5 inches. How many square inches of foil does he need?

_____

5 in.

Match the timeline events for the week with the correct year.

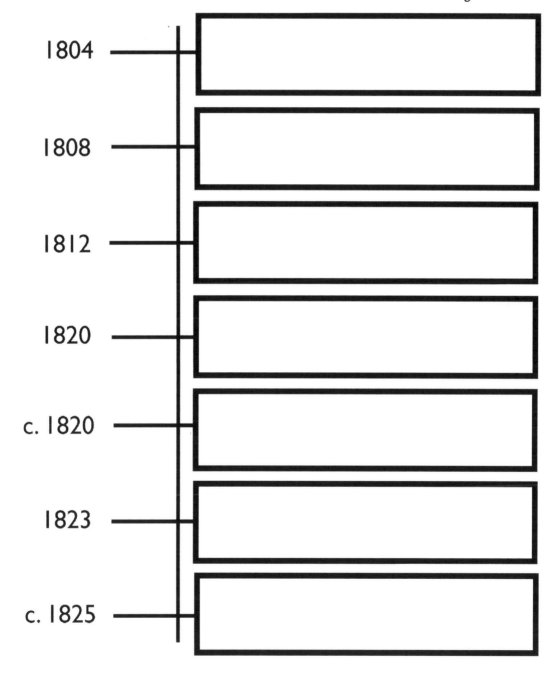

1804

1808

1812

1820

c. 1820

1823

c. 1825

Recite and memorize Newton's Second Law of Motion.
Label the picture below.

____ = ____ x ____

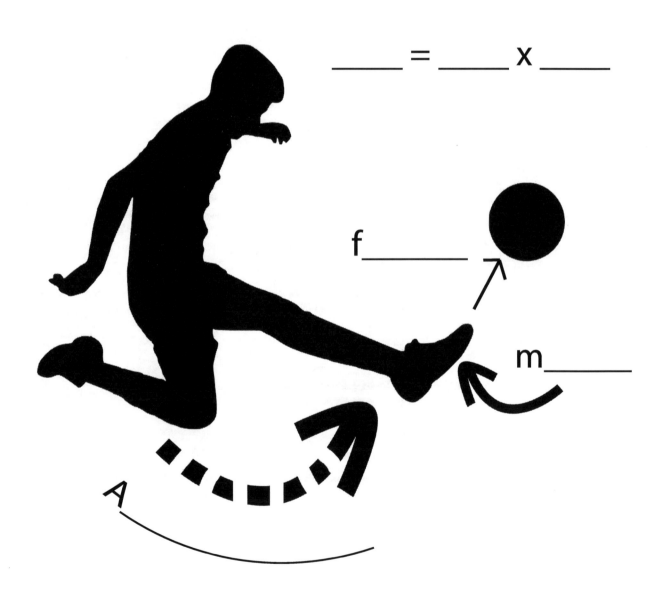

f_____

m_____

A_____

Research the science topic from this week. Write some notes below or draw a picture.

# REVIEW at a glance
## WEEK 17

## HISTORY
TELL ME ABOUT...

## TIMELINE
1.
2.
3.
4.
5.
6.
7.

## GEOGRAPHY
1.
2.
3.
4.
5.

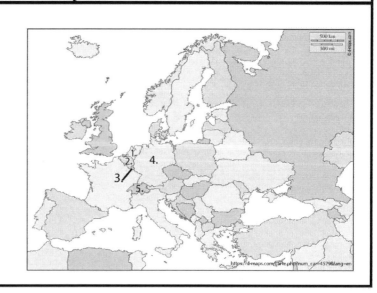

# REVIEW at a glance
## WEEK 17

**SCIENCE:** What is Newton's Second Law of Motion?

**MATH:** What is the area of a square?

**ENGLISH:** What is a noun?

**LATIN:**

| | singular | |
|---|---|---|
| | _____ | I shall _ |
| | _____ | you will _ |
| | _____ | he, she, it will _ |

| | plural | |
|---|---|---|
| | _____ | we shall _ |
| | _____ | you will _ |
| | _____ | they will _ |

# Week
18

# Journaling
date:

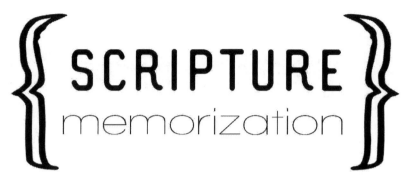

Find a verse in the Bible in your translation of choice.
Write it, say it, pray it, and memorize it.

**WRITE IT:** _____

_____

_____

_____

**SAY IT.**

**PRAY IT.**

**WRITE IT AGAIN (FROM MEMORY)** _____

_____

_____

_____

## Noun Cases

Fill in the blanks and match the kind of noun to the correct definition.

1. S_____

   tells to whom or for whom something is done

2. D_____ O_____

   the noun that follows a preposition

3. I_____ O_____

   the noun that performs the action in the sentence

4. O_____ of the P_____

   noun that tells us who owns or has something

5. P_____

   the noun that receives the action in the sentence

Fill in the blanks for the history sentence this week and copy it below.

Tell me about the _____ _____.

In _____, after the _____ of _____ failed to _____ _____ ____ II, _____ _____ _____, _____ _____ _____ _____, and _____ _____ _____ began the _____ _____.

_____

_____

_____

_____

_____

_____

Research the history topic from this week. Write some notes below or draw a picture.

Write the geography locations of the week below.
Color the map to mark each location.

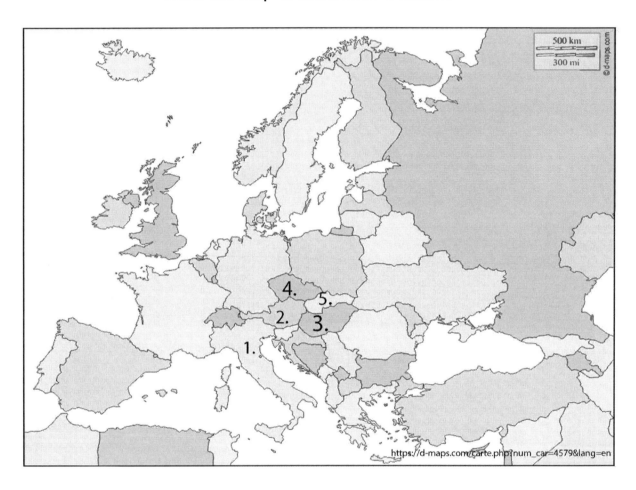

1.

2.

3.

4.

5.

# Math
## week 18

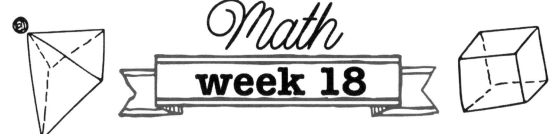

Fill in the blanks below.

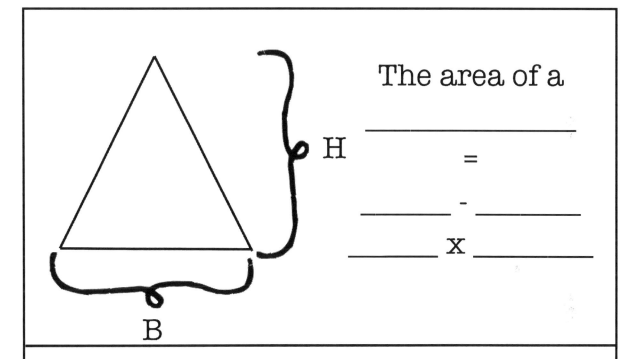

The area of a
_____
=
_____ · _____
_____ x _____

### Real Life Problem:

There is a small triangle part on Frank's house that needs to be painted. If the base is 10 feet and the height is 20 feet, determine the area of the part needing to be painted.

_____

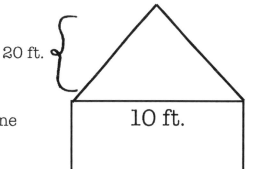

20 ft.

10 ft.

  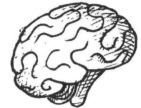

## 1st Conjugation Endings
## Future Tense

Sing the Latin Song for the week as you fill in the blanks

| singular | _____ | I shall _ |
| | _____ | you will _ |
| | _____ | he, she, it will _ |
| plural | _____ | we shall _ |
| | _____ | you will _ |
| | _____ | they will _ |

Match the timeline events for the week with the correct year.

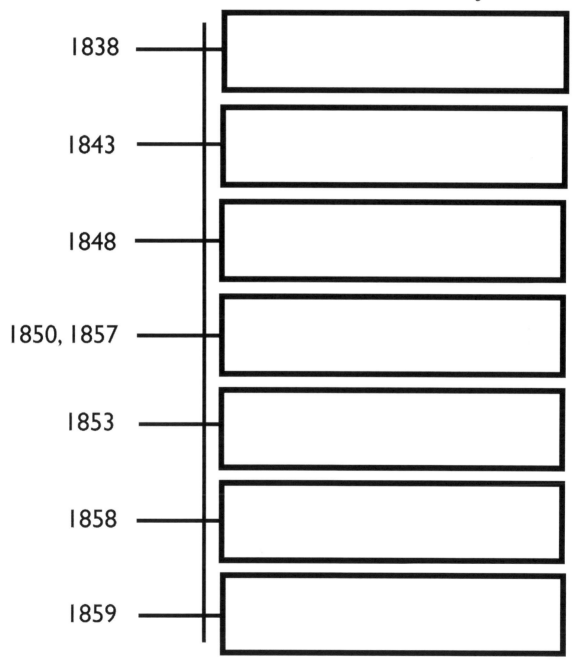

1838

1843

1848

1850, 1857

1853

1858

1859

# SCIENCE
## Newton's Laws of Motion

Recite and memorize Newton's Third Law of Motion.
Fill in the blanks and draw your own picture to describe.

For _____ action,

there is an _____ and

_____ _____.

Research the science topic from this week. Write some notes below or draw a picture.

# REVIEW at a glance
## WEEK 18

**HISTORY**
TELL ME ABOUT...

**TIMELINE**
1.
2.
3.
4.
5.
6.
7.

**GEOGRAPHY**
1.
2.
3.
4.
5.

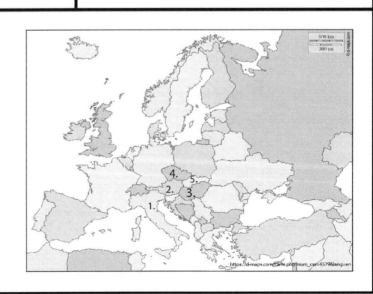

# REVIEW at a glance
## WEEK 18

**SCIENCE**: What is Newton's Third Law of Motion?

**MATH**: What is the area of a triangle?

**ENGLISH**: What are five cases of nouns?

**LATIN**:

|  | singular |  | |
|---|---|---|---|
|  | ___ | I shall _ | |
|  | ___ | you will _ | |
|  | ___ | he, she, it will _ | |
|  | plural |  | |
|  | ___ | we shall _ | |
|  | ___ | you will _ | |
|  | ___ | they will _ | |

# Week 19

# Journaling

date:

Find a verse in the Bible in your translation of choice.
Write it, say it, pray it, and memorize it.

**WRITE IT:** _____
_____
_____
_____

**SAY IT.**

**PRAY IT.**

**WRITE IT AGAIN (FROM MEMORY)** _____
_____
_____
_____

## GERUND

Fill in the blanks to make the definition of a gerund.

A _____ is a

_____ _____

_____ form _____

\_\_\_ a _____.

..............................................................

example (gerund in **bold**):

**Fishing** is really fun!

**Swimming** in the ocean has been Sally's favorite thing to do since she was a little girl.

**Eating** ice cream is wonderful on a hot day.

Fill in the blanks for the history sentence this week and copy it below.

**Tell me about the** _____ _____.

In _____, _____ _____ _____ led _____ _____ _____ to stop _____ _____ _____ from _____ all of _____ _____ during the _____ _____.

_____

_____

_____

_____

_____

_____

# 1st Conjugation Endings
# Present Perfect Tense

Sing the Latin Song for the week as you fill in the blanks

| singular | _____ _____ _____ | I have __ed<br>you have __ed<br>he, she, it has __ed |
|---|---|---|
| plural | _____ _____ _____ | we have __ed<br>you have __ed<br>they have __ed |

# Math
## week 19

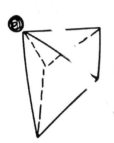

Fill in the blanks below.

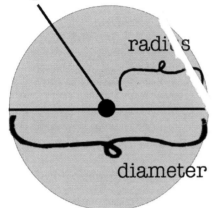

midpoint
radius
diameter

The area of a
_____
=
____ ( ___ . ___ )
x
the ____ _____
_____

### Real Life Problem:

Draw your favorite pizza toppings on this circle. If the radius of your pizza is 6 inches, what is the area?
_____

Match the timeline events for the week with the correct year.

1861

1865

1867

1871

1881

1898

c. 1900

# SCIENCE
## Laws of Thermodynamics

Recite and memorize the first law of thermodynamics.
Fill in the blanks below.

_____ cannot be

_____ or

_____

Research the science topic from this week. Write some notes below or draw a picture.

# REVIEW at a glance
## WEEK 19

### HISTORY
TELL ME ABOUT...

### TIMELINE
1.
2.
3.
4.
5.
6.
7.

### GEOGRAPHY
1.
2.
3.
4.
5.

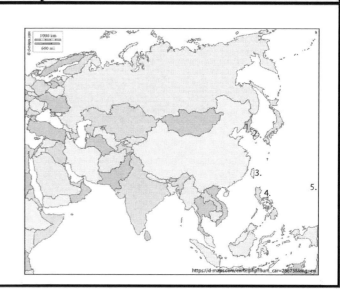

# REVIEW at a glance
## WEEK 19

**SCIENCE:** What is the first law of thermodynamics?

**MATH:** What is the area of a circle?

**ENGLISH:** What is a gerund?

**LATIN:**

| | | |
|---|---|---|
| singular | _____ | I have __ed |
| | _____ | you have __ed |
| | _____ | he, she, it has __ed |
| plural | _____ | we have __ed |
| | _____ | you have __ed |
| | _____ | they have __ed |

# Week 20

# Journaling
date:

Find a verse in the Bible in your translation of choice.
Write it, say it, pray it, and memorize it.

**WRITE IT:** _____

_____

_____

_____

**SAY IT.**

**PRAY IT.**

**WRITE IT AGAIN (FROM MEMORY)** _____

_____

_____

_____

## APPOSITIVE

Arrange the words in the key below to make the definition of an appositive.

An _____ is a _____ (or _____) directly _____ another _____ that explains ____ _____ it.

example (appositive in **bold**): Yesterday my teacher, **Mrs. Day**, laughed at my joke.
Pam, our **waitress**, was so kind to give us free dessert!
The last house, **the smaller grey house**, was sold.

..........................................................................

identifies   pronoun
beside   or   appositive
noun   noun

Fill in the blanks for the history sentence this week and copy it below.

Tell me about the _____ _____.

In _____, _____ _____ sent ___ _____ to stop _____ _____ _____ from capturing all of _____ _____ during the _____ _____.

_____

_____

_____

_____

_____

_____

_____

Research the history topic from this week. Write some notes below or draw a picture.

Write the geography locations of the week below.
Color the map to mark each location.

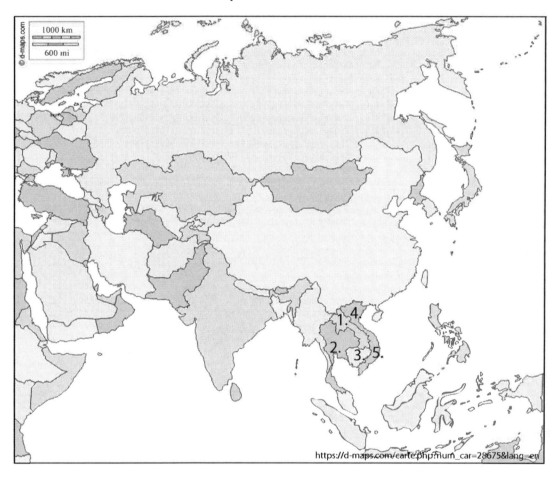

1.

2.

3.

4.

5.

  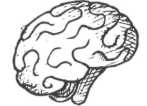

# 1st Conjugation Endings
# Present Perfect Tense

Sing the Latin Song for the week as you fill in the blanks

| singular | ___ ___ ___ | I have __ed<br>you have __ed<br>he, she, it has __ed |
|---|---|---|
| plural | ___ ___ ___ | we have __ed<br>you have __ed<br>they have __ed |

# Math week 20

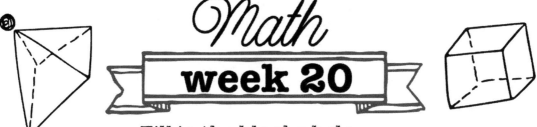

Fill in the blanks below.

midpoint

radius

diameter

circumference

TIP: Circumference is the name we use for circles to talk about the distance around the circle (instead of the word "perimeter" that we use for polygons).

The _____

of a _____

=

_____ x

____ ( ___.___ ___ )

x

the _____

## Real Life Problem:

Decorate this circle like the top of a cake. If the radius of the top of your cake is 4 inches, what is the circumference?

_____

# Timeline
## week 20

Match the timeline events for the week with the correct year.

1901

1910

1914

1917

1918

1920

1929

# SCIENCE
## Laws of Thermodynamics

Recite and memorize what the second law of thermodynamics explains. Write it in below.

_____

_____

_____

_____

_____

Research the science topic from this week. Write some notes below or draw a picture.

# REVIEW at a glance
## WEEK 20

**HISTORY**
TELL ME ABOUT...

**TIMELINE**
1.
2.
3.
4.
5.
6.
7.

**GEOGRAPHY**
1.
2.
3.
4.
5.

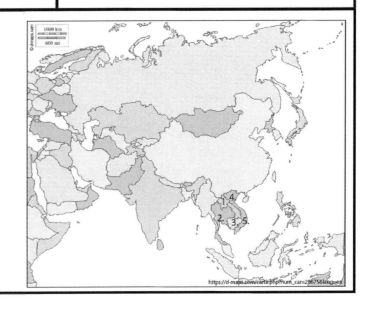

# REVIEW at a glance
## WEEK 20

**SCIENCE** — What is the second law of thermodynamics?

**MATH** — What is the circumference of a circle?

**ENGLISH** — What is an appositive?

**LATIN**

| | singular | |
|---|---|---|
| | _____ | I have __ed |
| | _____ | you have __ed |
| | _____ | he, she, it has __ed |

| | plural | |
|---|---|---|
| | _____ | we have __ed |
| | _____ | you have __ed |
| | _____ | they have __ed |

# Week 21

# Journaling
date:

Find a verse in the Bible in your translation of choice.
Write it, say it, pray it, and memorize it.

**WRITE IT:** _____

_____

_____

_____

**SAY IT.**

**PRAY IT.**

**WRITE IT AGAIN (FROM MEMORY)** _____

_____

_____

_____

_____

## CONJUNCTION

What is the definition of a conjunction?

A _____ is a _____ to _____ words, _____, or _____ together.

........................................................

**Circle the Conjunction:**

She took the ham and cheese sandwhich.

We walked fast, and we jumped for joy.

She was happy, yet she cried.

They came early, so we served them lunch.

Would you like pizza or spaghetti?

Fill in the blanks for the history sentence this week and copy it below.

Tell me about the _____ of the _____ _____.

In the _____, _____ _____ _____ _____ _____ and _____ _____ _____ _____ worked together to end the _____ _____, _____ big _____ , and _____ the _____ _____ .

_____
_____
_____
_____
_____
_____
_____

Research the history topic from this week. Write some notes below or draw a picture.

Write the geography locations of the week below.
Find them on the map and draw a line to match it.

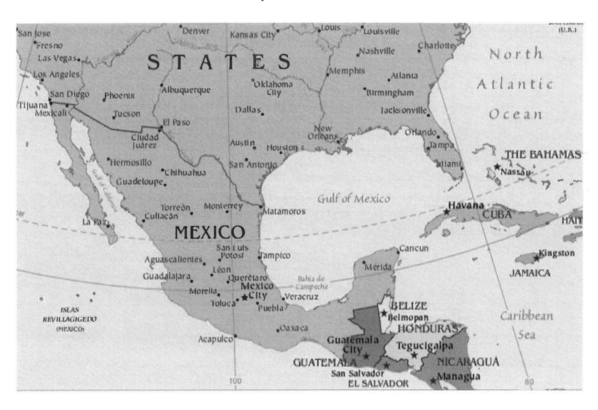

1.

2.

3.

4.

5.

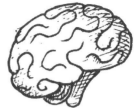

# 1st Conjugation Endings
# Pluperfect Tense

Sing the Latin Song for the week as you fill in the blanks

| singular | _____<br>_____<br>_____ | I had __ed<br>you had __ed<br>he, she, it had __ed |
|---|---|---|
| plural | _____<br>_____<br>_____ | we had __ed<br>you had __ed<br>they had __ed |

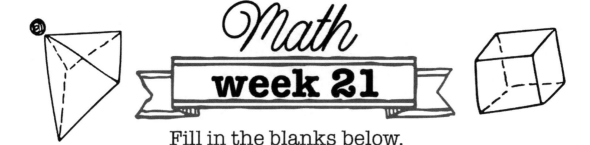

Fill in the blanks below.

## The Associative Law for Addition

$$( \_ + \_ ) + \_ = \_ + ( \_ + \_ )$$

If a=5, b=3, and c=2 it would look like this:

$$( 5 + 3 ) + 2 = 5 + ( 3 + 2 )$$

solved: 10=10

Now, recreate your own number sentences below:

$$(\_ + \_) + \_ = \_ + (\_ + \_)$$
$$\_ = \_$$

$$(\_ + \_) + \_ = \_ + (\_ + \_)$$
$$\_ = \_$$

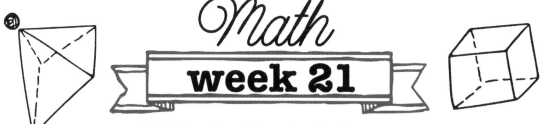

Math week 21

Fill in the blanks below.

## The Associative Law for Multiplication

$$( \_ \times \_ ) \times \_ = \_ \times ( \_ \times \_ )$$

If a=5, b=3, and c=2 it would look like this:

$$( 5 \times 3 ) \times 2 = 5 \times ( 3 \times 2 )$$

solved: 30=30

Now, recreate your own number sentences below:

$$( \_ \times \_ ) \times \_ = \_ \times ( \_ \times \_ )$$
$$\_\_ = \_\_$$

$$( \_ \times \_ ) \times \_ = \_ \times ( \_ \times \_ )$$
$$\_\_ = \_\_$$

Match the timeline events for the week with the correct year.

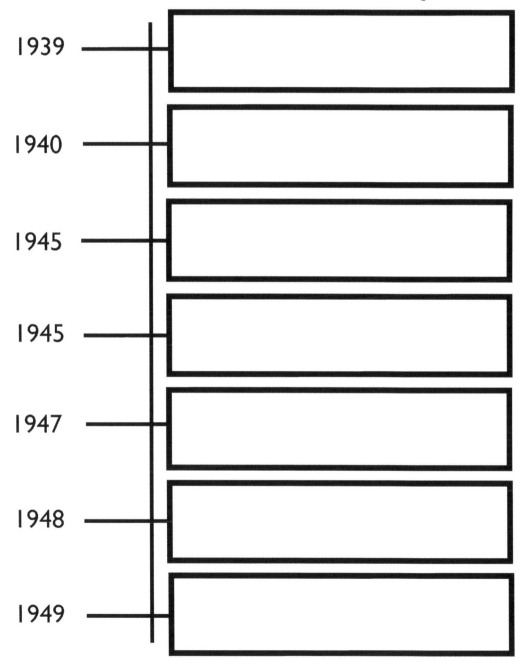

1939

1940

1945

1945

1947

1948

1949

# SCIENCE
## Laws of Thermodynamics

Recite and memorize what the third law of thermodynamics explains. Write it in below.

_____

_____

_____

_____

_____

Research the science topic from this week. Write some notes below or draw a picture.

_____

# REVIEW at a glance
## WEEK 21

## HISTORY
TELL ME ABOUT...

## TIMELINE
1.
2.
3.
4.
5.
6.
7.

## GEOGRAPHY
1.
2.
3.
4.
5.

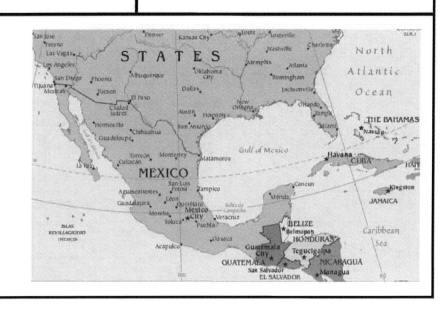

# REVIEW at a glance
## WEEK 21

**SCIENCE** What is the third law of thermodynamics?

**MATH** What is the Associative Law for addition and multiplication?

**ENGLISH** What is a conjunction?

**LATIN**

| singular | | |
|---|---|---|
| | _____ | I had __ed |
| | _____ | you had __ed |
| | _____ | he, she, it had __ed |

| plural | | |
|---|---|---|
| | _____ | we had __ed |
| | _____ | you had __ed |
| | _____ | they had __ed |

# Week
## 22

# Journaling
date:

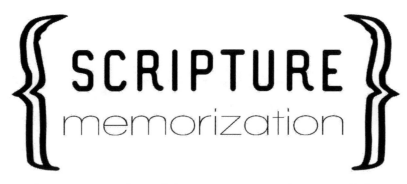

Find a verse in the Bible in your translation of choice.
Write it, say it, pray it, and memorize it.

**WRITE IT:** _____

_____

_____

_____


**SAY IT.**

**PRAY IT.**

**WRITE IT AGAIN (FROM MEMORY)** _____

_____

_____

_____

## COORDINATING CONJUNCTIONS

Fill in the correct coordinating conjunctions and then find them three times each in the word search.

F _ _

A _ _

N _ _

B _ _

O _

Y _ _

S _

```
N H R T Q F O S Z D N
E X U O O W T R O O T
S O R R O R E K J C R
W J N O S O Y F O S G
F O M A N F O N M R B
R F N Y G R O B I X Q
F D T A E R U K D V M
N X E N D T X N G R P
Q G Y D Y R A K V P C
T U B T U B G R N E Y
S Y J X P G M R F U C
```

Fill in the blanks for the history sentence this week and copy it below.

Tell me about the _____ of _____.

In _____, the _____ _____ began to fall in _____ _____ when _____ _____ _____ _____ refused to send them _____ _____.

_____
_____
_____
_____
_____
_____
_____

Research the history topic from this week. Write some notes below or draw a picture.

Write the geography locations of the week below.
Find them on the map and draw a line to match it.

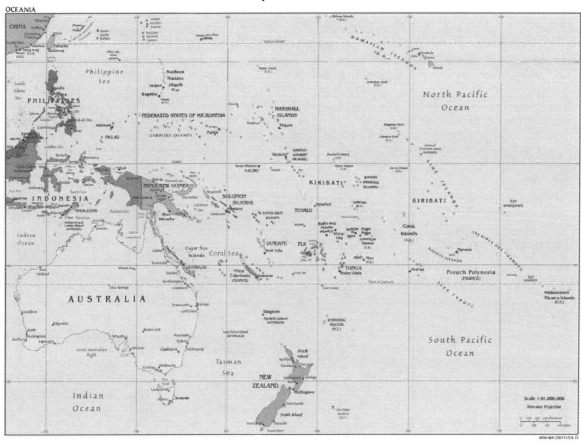

1.

2.

3.

4.

5.

## 1st Conjugation Endings
## Pluperfect Tense

Sing the Latin Song for the week as you fill in the blanks

| singular | | |
|---|---|---|
| | _____ | I had __ed |
| | _____ | you had __ed |
| | _____ | he, she, it had __ed |

| plural | | |
|---|---|---|
| | _____ | we had __ed |
| | _____ | you had __ed |
| | _____ | they had __ed |

# Math
## week 22

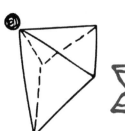 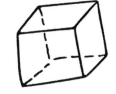

Fill in the blanks below.

## The Commutative Law for Addition

__ + __ = __ + __

If a = 9 and b = 7, it would look like this:

$$9+7 = 7+9$$

solved, 16=16

---

Now, recreate your own number sentences below:

__ + __ = __ + __      __ + __ = __ + __

__ = __                __ = __

__ + __ = __ + __      __ + __ = __ + __

__ = __                __ = __

# Math
## week 22

Fill in the blanks below.

### The Commutative Law for Multiplication

_ X _ = _ X _

If a = 5 and b = 4, it would look like this:

## 5x4 = 4x5

solved, 20=20

---

Now, recreate your own number sentences below:

_X_ = _X_  |  _X_ = _X_
_ = _     |   _ = _

_X_ = _X_  |  _X_ = _X_
_ = _     |   _ = _

Match the timeline events for the week with the correct year.

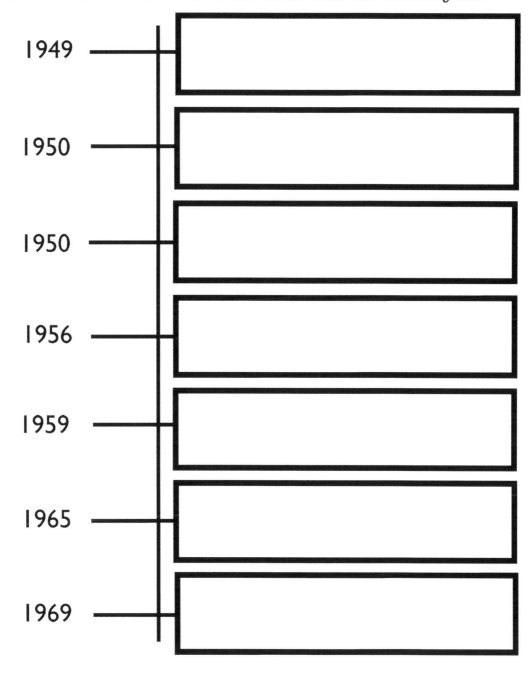

1949

1950

1950

1956

1959

1965

1969

# SCIENCE Light

Light can be observed in many different ways.
Write in the missing words to match the diagram.

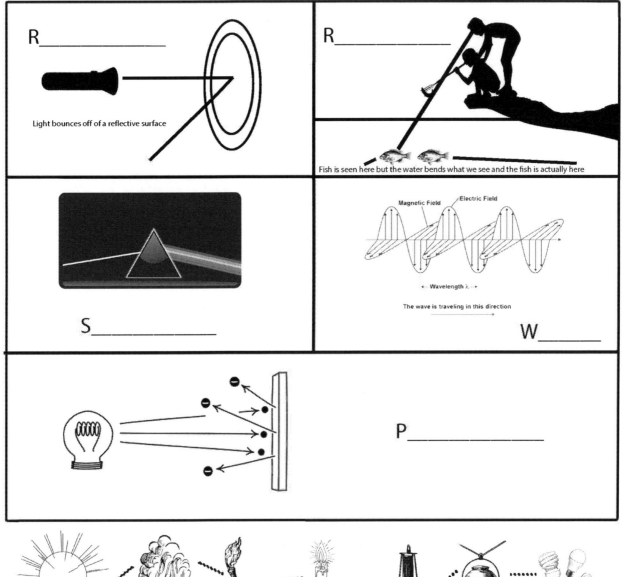

R_____ — Light bounces off of a reflective surface

R_____ — Fish is seen here but the water bends what we see and the fish is actually here

S_____

W_____

P_____

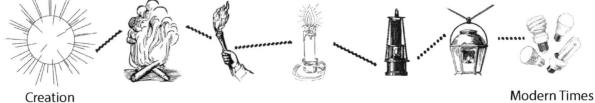

Creation                                        Modern Times

Research the science topic from this week. Write some notes below or draw a picture.

# {REVIEW at a glance}
## WEEK 22

## HISTORY
TELL ME ABOUT...

## TIMELINE
1.
2.
3.
4.
5.
6.
7.

## GEOGRAPHY
1.
2.
3.
4.
5.

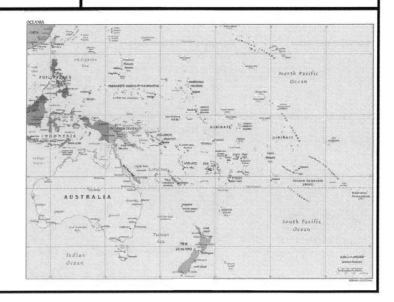

# REVIEW at a glance
## WEEK 22

**SCIENCE**
What are some ways light is observed?

**MATH**
What is the Commutative Law for addition and multiplication?

**ENGLISH**
What are the coordinating conjunctions?

**LATIN**

| | singular | | |
|---|---|---|---|
| | _____ | I had __ed | |
| | _____ | you had __ed | |
| | _____ | he, she, it had __ed | |

| | plural | | |
|---|---|---|---|
| | _____ | we had __ed | |
| | _____ | you had __ed | |
| | _____ | they had __ed | |

# Week 23

# Journaling
date:

Find a verse in the Bible in your translation of choice.
Write it, say it, pray it, and memorize it.

**WRITE IT:** _____

_____

_____

_____

**SAY IT.**

**PRAY IT.**

**WRITE IT AGAIN (FROM MEMORY)** _____

_____

_____

_____

## ADJECTIVE

Fill in the blanks to make the definition of an adjective.

An _____ _____ a _____ or _____ by _____ , _____, or _____ - And answers the questions: What _____? How _____? _____? _____?

# HISTORY
## week 23

Fill in the blanks for the history sentence this week and copy it below.

Tell me about the _____ _____.

In _____, _____ _____ H.W. _____ sent _____ to the _____ _____ to _____ _____ _____ _____ _____ from _____ during the _____ _____.

_____

_____

_____

_____

_____

_____

Research the history topic from this week. Write some notes below or draw a picture.

Write the geography locations of the week below.
Color the map to mark each location.

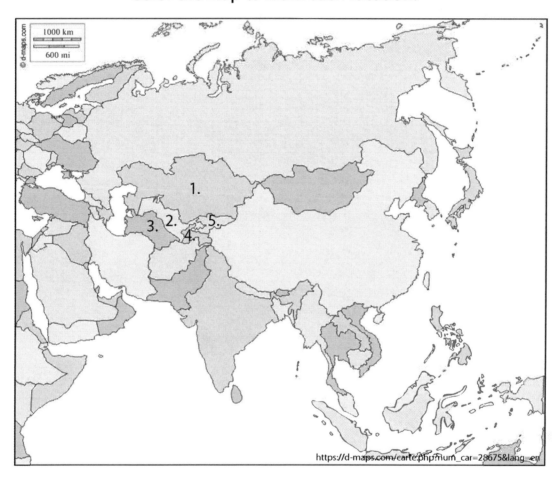

1.

2.

3.

4.

5.

  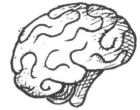

# 1st Conjugation Endings
# Future Perfect Tense

Sing the Latin Song for the week as you fill in the blanks

| singular | | |
|---|---|---|
| | _____ | I shall have \_\_\_ed |
| | _____ | you will have \_\_\_ed |
| | _____ | he, she, it had \_\_\_ed |
| **plural** | _____ | we shall have \_\_\_ed |
| | _____ | you will have \_\_\_ed |
| | _____ | they will have \_\_\_ed |

# Math
## week 23

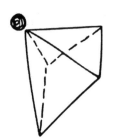 

Fill in the blanks below.

## The Distributive Law

$$\_\,(\_ + \_) = (\_ \times \_) + (\_ \times \_)$$

If a = 1, b = 2, and c = 3 it would look like this:

$$1 \times (2+3) = (1 \times 2) + (1 \times 3)$$

First, solve the parentheses.   $1 \times 5 = 2+3$

solved: $5 = 5$

---

Now, recreate your own number sentences below.

$$\_\,(\_ + \_) = (\_ \times \_) + (\_ \times \_)$$

$$\_ = \_$$

$$\_\,(\_ + \_) = (\_ \times \_) + (\_ \times \_)$$

$$\_ = \_$$

Match the timeline events for the week with the correct year.

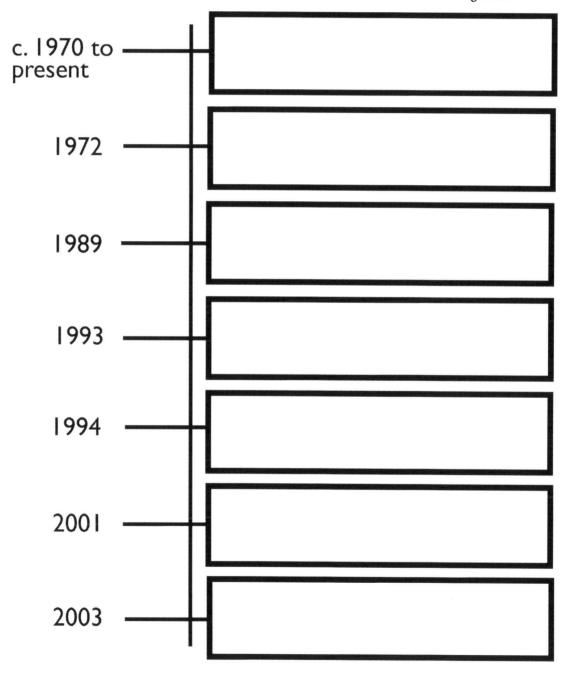

c. 1970 to present

1972

1989

1993

1994

2001

2003

Fill in the blanks with the ways heat transfer.

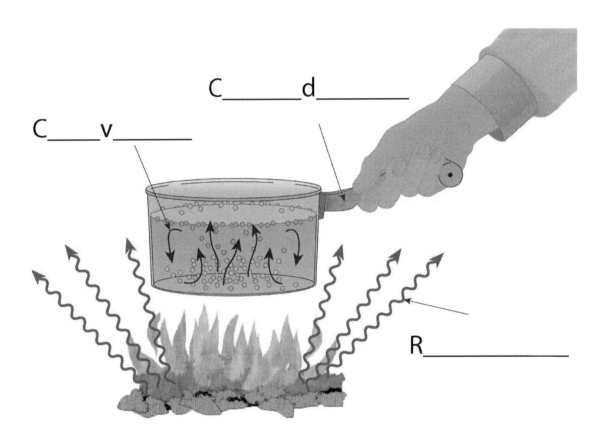

C\_\_\_\_d_____

C\_\_\_\_v_____

R_____

# HEAT WILL FLOW AS LONG AS ONE TEMPERATURE IS HIGHER THAN THE OTHER.

Research the science topic from this week. Write some notes below or draw a picture.

# REVIEW at a glance
## WEEK 23

**HISTORY**
TELL ME ABOUT...

**TIMELINE**
1.
2.
3.
4.
5.
6.
7.

**GEOGRAPHY**
1.
2.
3.
4.
5.

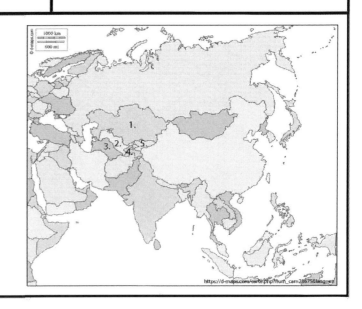

# REVIEW at a glance
## WEEK 23

**SCIENCE** — How does heat flow?

**MATH** — What is the Distributive Law?

**ENGLISH** — What is an Adjective?

**LATIN**

| | singular | |
|---|---|---|
| | _____ | I shall have \_\_\_ed |
| | _____ | you will have \_\_\_ed |
| | _____ | he, she, it had \_\_\_ed |

| | plural | |
|---|---|---|
| | _____ | we shall have \_\_\_ed |
| | _____ | you will have \_\_\_ed |
| | _____ | they will have \_\_\_ed |

# Week 24

# Journaling
date:

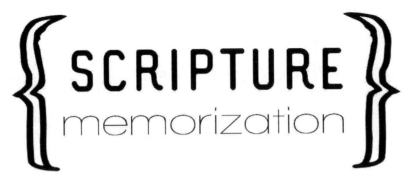

Find a verse in the Bible in your translation of choice.
Write it, say it, pray it, and memorize it.

**WRITE IT:** _____

_____

_____

_____

**SAY IT.**

**PRAY IT.**

**WRITE IT AGAIN (FROM MEMORY)** _____

_____

_____

_____

_____

## INTERJECTION

Fill in the blanks to make the definition of an interjection.

An _____ is a _____ or _____ used as a _____ _____ of _____ or _____.

..............................................

**Write some interjections in the comic bubbles:**

Fill in the blanks for the history sentence this week and copy it below.

Tell me about the _____ of _____.

In _____, _____ _____ _____ de _____ allowed _____ _____. _____ _____ became _____ _____ _____ _____ _____ _____ _____ was _____ .

_____

_____

_____

_____

_____

_____

Research the history topic from this week. Write some notes below or draw a picture.

Write the geography locations of the week below.
Find them on the map and draw a line to match it.

1.

2.

3.

4.

5.

  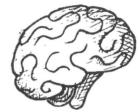

# 1st Conjugation Endings
# Future Perfect Tense

Sing the Latin Song for the week as you fill in the blanks

| | |
|---|---|
| singular _____ | I shall have ___ed |
| _____ | you will have ___ed |
| _____ | he, she, it had ___ed |
| plural _____ | we shall have ___ed |
| _____ | you will have ___ed |
| _____ | they will have ___ed |

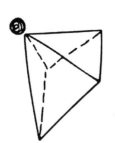 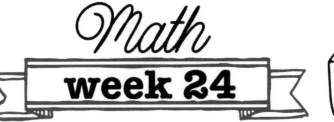 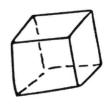

Fill in the blanks below.

## The Identity Law for Addition

__ + __ = __

If a = 5 it would look like this:

## 5+0=5

Basically, anything plus zero equals itself.

---

### Now, recreate your own number sentences below:

__ + ◯ =          __ + ◯ =

__ + ◯ =          __ + ◯ =

__ + ◯ =          __ + ◯ =

__ + ◯ =          __ + ◯ =

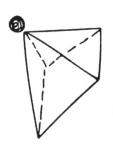 

# Math week 24

Fill in the blanks below.

## The Identity Law for Multiplication

__ x __ = __

If a = 23 it would look like this:

## 23x1=23

Basically, anything times one equals itself.

---

__ x 1 =

__ x 1 =

__ x 1 =

__ x 1 =

__ x 1 =

__ x 1 =

__ x 1 =

__ x 1 =

## PART 1
## U.S. Presidents
### Fact Activity

Match the US President to the correct fact!

(resources: http://www.mistergworld.com/12-002.htm, whitehouse.gov, NG for Kids)

| | |
|---|---|
| 1st - Washington | a. first to live in the White House |
| 2nd - John Adams | b. had 15 kids |
| 3rd - Jefferson | c. first president born a US citizen |
| 4th - Madison | d. 1st president to have stove in White House |
| 5th - Monroe | e. son of the second president |
| 6th - John Quincy Adams | f. memorized his first speech (3,319 words) |
| 7th - Jackson | g. teeth were made from elephant tusks |
| 8th - Van Buren | h. spoke 6 different languages |
| 9th - Harrison | i. president for only 31 days |
| 10th - Tyler | j. expanded the US to the west coast |
| 11th - Polk | k. died after eating bad cherries |
| 12th - Taylor | l. first president to ride in a train |
| 13th - Fillmore | m. smallest president |
| 14th - Pierce | n. had no opponent in the 1820 election |

key: 1-g 2-a 3-h 4-m 5-n 6-e 7-L 8-c 9-i 10-b 11-j 12-k 13-d 14-f

www.sunshineandoranges.com

## PART 2

Match the US President to the correct fact!

| | |
|---|---|
| 15th - Buchanan | a. first president to use a phone |
| 16th - Lincoln | b. dreamed of being a stage performer |
| 17th - Johnson | c. 1st to have Christmas tree in White House |
| 18th - Grant | d. changed his pants many times a day |
| 19th - Hayes | e. heaviest president |
| 20th - Garfield | f. fined $20 for speeding in his horse carriage |
| 21st - Arthur | g. never married |
| 22nd - Cleveland | h. 1st to marry in the White House |
| 23rd - Harrison | i. buried with a copy of the Constitution |
| 24th - Cleveland | j. 1st to use campaign buttons |
| 25th - McKinley | k. wrote with both hands at the same time |
| 26th - Theodore Roosevelt | l. youngest person ever to be president |
| 27th - Taft | m. tallest president |
| 28th - Wilson | n. 1st president to serve two non-consecutive terms |

key: 15-g 16-m 17-i 18-f 19-a 20-k 21-d 22-n 23-c 24-h 25-j 26-l 27-e 28-b

## PART 3
## U.S. Presidents
### Fact Activity

Match the US President to the correct fact!

29th - Harding          a. oldest president (age 69-77)

30th - Coolidge         b. auto mechanic before being president

31st - Hoover           c. 1st African-American president

32nd - Roosevelt        d. played the saxophone on national TV

33rd - Truman           e. held daughter's prom at the White House

34th - Eisenhower       f. died while serving as president

35th - Kennedy          g. survived 4 plane crashes in WWII

36th - Johnson          h. his nickname was "Silent Cal"

37th - Nixon            i. use to host reality TV show, "The Apprentice"

38th - Ford             j. only president to serve more than 2 terms

39th - Carter           k. commanded the Allied forces on "D-Day"

40th - Reagan           l. served during the Great Depression

41st - George Bush      m. has a collection of over 250 signed baseballs

42nd - Clinton          n. was assassinated in 1963

43rd - George W Bush    o. first president born in a hospital

44th - Obama            p. read every book in his hometown library

45th - Trump            q. born in California

key: 29-f 30-h 31-l 32-j 33-p 34-k 35-n 36-b 37-q 38-o 39-e 40-a 41-g 42-d 43-m 44-c 45-i

www.sunshineandoranges.com

Write in what each unit measures.

## $\Omega$ = ohms

What does it measure?

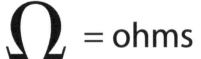 = volts

What does it measure?

 = amps

What does it measure?

## W = watts

What does it measure?

Research the science topic from this week. Write some notes below or draw a picture.

# REVIEW at a glance
## WEEK 24

**HISTORY**
TELL ME ABOUT...

**PRESIDENTS**

**GEOGRAPHY**

1.
2.
3.
4.
5.

 # REVIEW
at a glance
**WEEK 24**

**SCIENCE:** What units are used to measure electricity?

**MATH:** What is the Identity Law for addition and multiplication?

**ENGLISH:** What is an interjection?

**LATIN:**

| | singular | | |
|---|---|---|---|
| | _____ | I shall have ___ed |
| | _____ | you will have ___ed |
| | _____ | he, she, it had ___ed |

| | plural | | |
|---|---|---|---|
| | _____ | we shall have ___ed |
| | _____ | you will have ___ed |
| | _____ | they will have ___ed |

# Extras

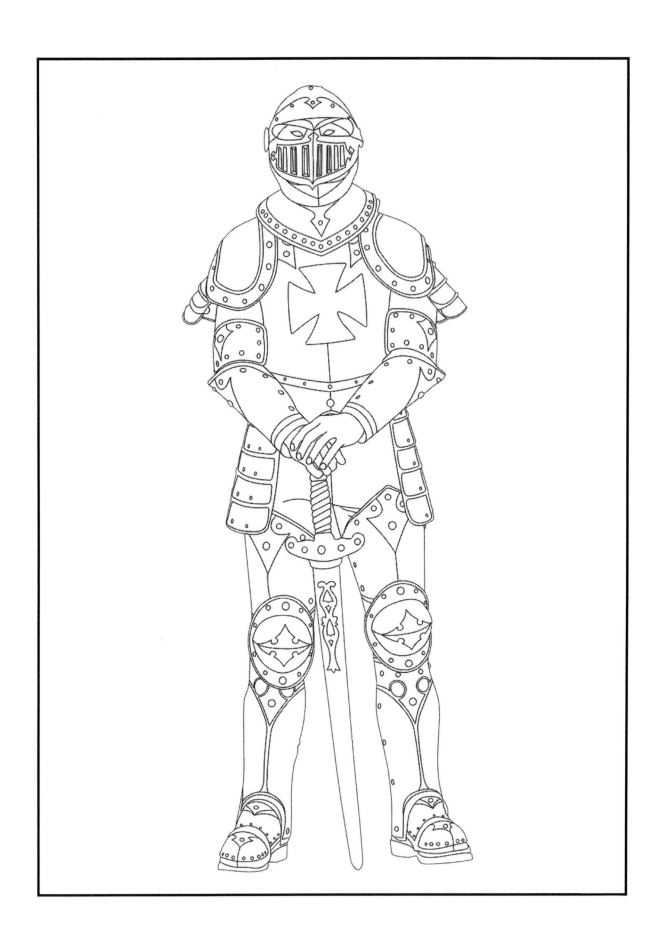

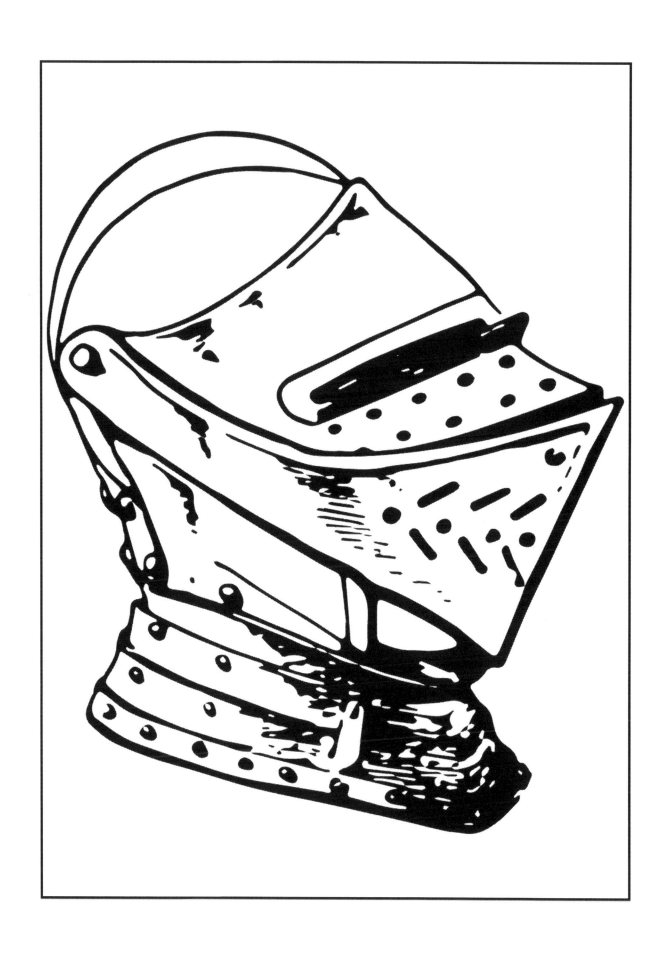

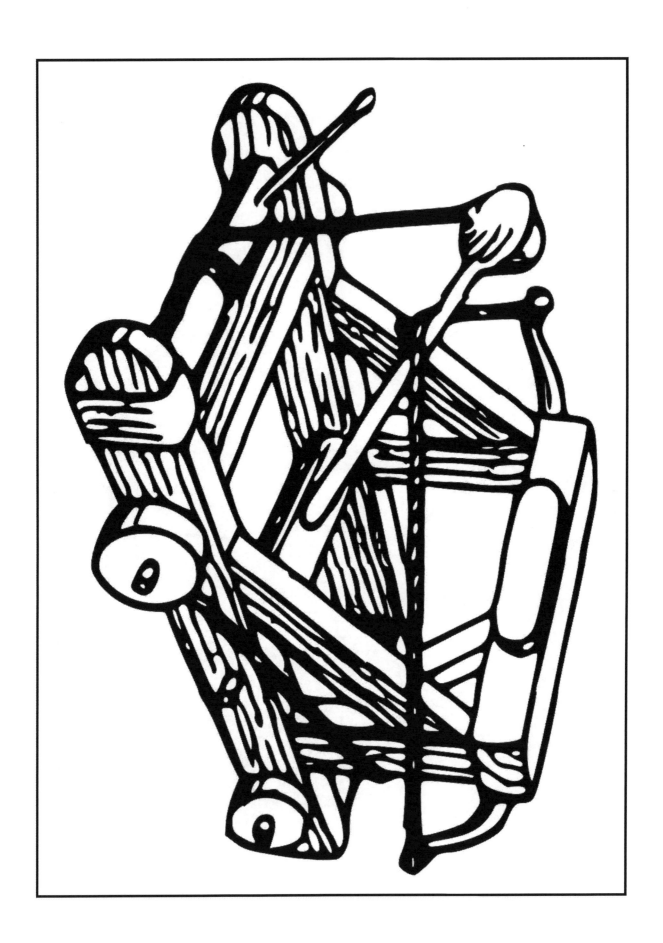

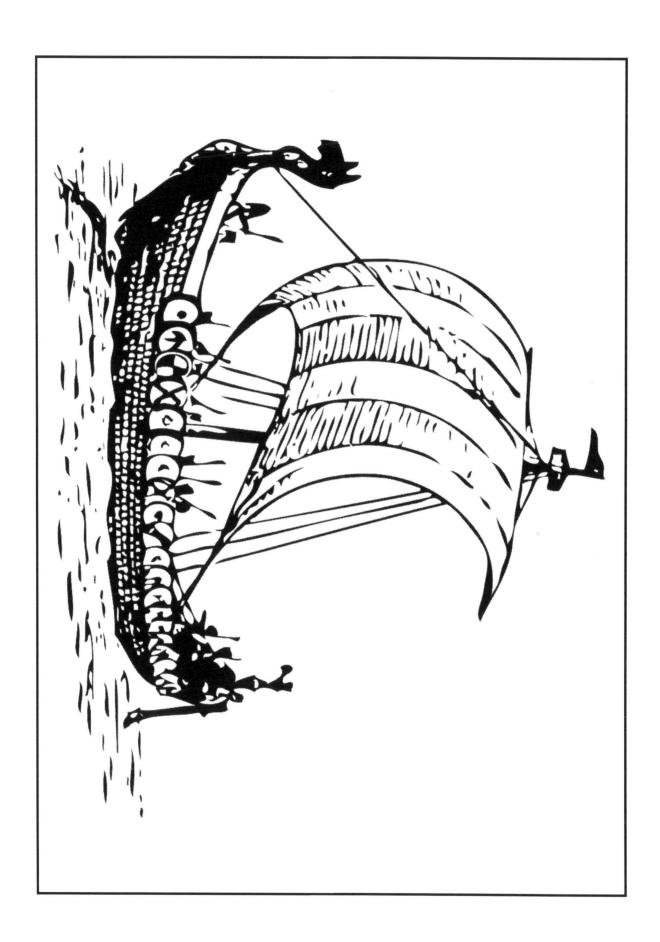

# Journaling
date:

# Journaling
date:

# Journaling
date:

# Journaling
date:

# Journaling
date:

# Journaling
date:

# Journaling

date:

# Journaling
date:

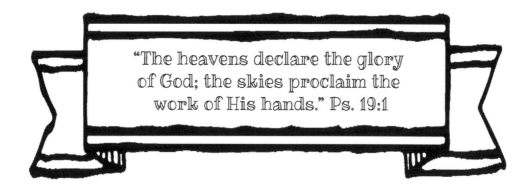

"The heavens declare the glory of God; the skies proclaim the work of His hands." Ps. 19:1

**Thank you** for your download! I hope my material can help your child and your journey with Classical Conversations. My children are the reason I created them and I wanted to find a way to pass them along to you.

A huge thank you to Classical Conversations for being such a wonderful choice for our own homeschooling journey. We love them so much we can't help but talk about them. They have been so gracious to us in the creation of these notebooks!

Thank you to my friends and family for being so supportive. Thank you to all of the amazing artists that have created the clip art and fonts that I have purchased to use in this notebook.

Ultimately, thank you Lord for the grace you have bestowed upon us! We certainly do not deserve it. It is our hope and goal that what we do ultimately brings glory to Him.

There are many creative mama's out there working hard to create great resources that work best for you and your family. If this resources doesn't work for you and your family there are so many others to try out. Don't be discouraged - lean into the Lord for guideance and support. Surely if He has called you to this homeschooling thing, He will also equip you for every possible thing coming your way.

For more homeschool related materials and downloads, as well as Bible study goodies for you and your home, you can visit my website:
www.sunshineandoranges.com
amy@sunshineandoranges.com

# Congratulations,

Write your name here.

**You finished with flying colors! Be proud and celebrate your accomplishments.**

This certificate of completion is presented to

_____ on the _____ day of _____

in the year _____.

_____        _____
date                                              teacher

Made in the USA
San Bernardino, CA
04 September 2019